The Essential
KAHLIL GIBRAN

The Essential

KAHLIL GIBRAN

Aphorisms and Maxims

EDITED BY JOSEPH SHEBAN

PHILOSOPHICAL
LIBRARY

CITADEL PRESS
Kensington Publishing Corp.
www.kensingtonbooks.com

CITADEL PRESS books are published by

Kensington Publishing Corp.
850 Third Avenue
New York, NY 10022

This title is published by arrangement with Philosophical Library. Previously published by Citadel Press/Philosophical Library under the title *The Wisdom of Gibran*.

All Kensington titles, imprints, and distributed lines are available at special quantity discounts for bulk purchases for sales promotions, premiums, fund raising, educational, or institutional use. Special book excerpts or customized printings can also be created to fit specific needs. For details, write or phone the office of the Kensington special sales manager: Kensington Publishing Corp., 850 Third Avenue, New York, NY 10022, attn: Special Sales Department; phone 1-800-221-2647.

First printing: September 2005

10 9 8 7 6 5 4 3 2

Printed in the United States of America

CIP data is available from the Library of Congress.

ISBN 0-8065-2715-3

To my children,
Jeneen, George and Faram,
I dedicate this work.

KEY

BW-ST: *Broken Wings* by Kahlil Gibran, in *A Second Treasury of Kahlil Gibran,* trans. by Anthony R. Ferris, Citadel Press, 1962.

KG-P: *Kahlil Gibran: A Biography* by Michael Naimy, in *The Parables of Gibran* by Annie Salem Otto, Citadel Press, 1963.

P: *The Procession* by Kahlil Gibran, trans. by George Kheirallah, Philosophical Library, 1958.

MS: *Mirrors of the Soul, Kahlil Gibran,* by Joseph Sheban, Philosophical Library, 1965.

S: In conversation and correspondence.

SH-P: *Secrets of the Heart* by Kahlil Gibran in *The Parables of Gibran.*

SH-T: *Secrets of the Heart* by Kahlil Gibran in *A Treasury of Kahlil Gibran,* trans. by Anthony Rizcallah Ferris, edited by Martin L. Wolf, Citadel Press, 1947.

SP-P: *Kahlil Gibran: A Self Portrait,* trans. by Anthony R. Ferris, in *The Parables of Gibran.*

SR-T: *Spirits Rebellious* by Kahlil Gibran in *A Treasury of Kahlil Gibran.*

T: *A Treasury of Kahlil Gibran.*

TL-T: *Tears and Laughter* by Kahlil Gibran in *A Treasury of Kahlil Gibran.*

VM-P: *The Voice of the Master* by Kahlil Gibran in *The Parables of Gibran.*

WM-ST: *The Words of the Master* by Kahlil Gibran in *A Second Treasury of Kahlil Gibran.*

INTRODUCTION

Khalil Gibran, whose books have been international best-sellers for more than fifty years, was born near the Holy Cedars of Lebanon. While Khalil was a young boy, his family migrated to the United States. After several years in Boston schools, Gibran's family sent him back to Lebanon to be educated at a college in Beirut. Later, he was sent to Paris for further education. Gibran then returned to the United States, where he applied his brush to painting and his pen to writing in Arabic. Through his first art exhibit, in Boston, he met Miss Mary Haskell, who became patron of his further art studies in Paris.

Because of his cosmopolitan background and education, Khalil became first a student of and then an interpreter of the Middle East, Europe and America. Thus, through him, the twain, East and West in great fulfillment, met. He brought to his readers of Arabic the simplicity of English expression, a refreshing freedom of thought and a frankness which demanded reform. In Arabic, his style and concepts were revolutionary. To his readers in English, he brought the poetry, family traditions, sagacity and philosophy of the Middle East: the great sweep of Christianity, Islam and Judaism, as well as their ancient roots.

Khalil Gibran's songs were of the earth; he loved his fellow man, to whom he carried the torch of freedom for all peoples alike:

"I love you, my Brother," he wrote, "wherever you are, whether you kneel in your church, worship in your synagogue or pray in your mosque."

Gibran's essays, poems and stories are salted with nuggets of wisdom; thus his writing, although simple, is unique and immortal. Within the covers of this work there is a collection of those nuggets, reflecting his philosophy and his unique expression. For example, in a love story, he wrote:

"The first kiss is the beginning of the Song of Life. It is a word uttered by four lips proclaiming the heart as a throne and love as a king. It is the first flower at the tip of the branch of the tree of life."

Writing of government, he urged, long before John F. Kennedy was to repeat his words: "Ask not what your country can do for you, but ask what you can do for your country."

Of tyrants, he wrote: "You may chain my hands, you may shackle my feet; you may even throw me into a dark prison; but you shall not enslave my thinking, because it is free."

As a young man in Lebanon, Khalil Gibran loved a beautiful girl, but her parents refused their permission for marriage because of Khalil's poverty. Later, through letters they exchanged, Gibran came to love another woman, but he was too poor and too ill to travel to Lebanon to marry her. Yet the paradox is that, though Gibran lost the two loves of his life because of his poverty, his books have earned more than two million dollars in royalties.

Gibran lived all his mature life in a small, fourth-floor walk-up studio in New York but he dreamed always of returning to the beautiful mountains of Lebanon, the homeland of his heart which he described thus:

"Lebanon, among Western poets, is an imaginary place whose real existance vanished with the passing of David, Solomon and the Prophets, as the Garden of Eden was hidden through the fall of Adam and Eve. Lebanon is a poetical expression and not the name of a mountain."

And:

"Spring is beautiful everywhere, but it is more than beautiful in Lebanon. Spring is the spirit of an unknown God speeding through the world, which, as it reaches Lebanon, pauses, because now it is as at home with the souls of the Prophets and Kings hovering over the land, chanting with the brooks of Judea the eternal Psalms of Solomon, renewing with the Cedars of Lebanon memories of an ancient glory."

The body of Khalil Gibran now rests in the shadow of the Holy Cedars, his soul, as his Spring in Lebanon, hovering and chanting, in his own words:

"The river continues on its way to the sea, broken the wheel of the mill or not."

Joseph Sheban
5020 Sheban Drive
Youngstown, Ohio

A

Action

A little knowledge that *acts* is worth infinitely more than much knowledge that is idle.

—WM-ST-63

Believing is a fine thing, but placing those beliefs into execution is a test of strength. Many are those who talk like the roar of the sea, but their lives are shallow and stagnant, like the rotting marshes. Many are those who lift their heads above the mountain tops, but their spirits remain dormant in the obscurity of the caverns.

—SH-T-17

Adolescence

It is said that unsophistication makes a man empty and that emptiness makes him carefree. It may be true among those who were born dead and who exist like frozen corpses; but the sensitive boy who feels much and knows little is the most unfortunate creature under the sun, because he is torn by two forces. The first force elevates him and shows him the beauty of existence through a cloud of dreams; the second ties him down to the earth and fills his eyes with dust and overpowers him with fears and darkness.

—BW-ST-18

Advice

He who does not seek advice is a fool. His folly blinds him to Truth and makes him evil, stubborn, and a danger to his fellow man.

—WM-ST-67

Affection

The heart's affections are divided like the branches of the cedar tree; if the tree loses one strong branch, it will suffer but it does not die. It will pour all its vitality into the next branch so that it will grow and fill the empty place.

—BW-ST-93

Age

Seek ye counsel of the aged, for their eyes have looked on the faces of the years and their ears have hearkened to the voices of Life. Even if their counsel is displeasing to you, pay heed to them.

—WM-ST-68

Ambition

What good is there, pray thee tell me,
        In jostling through the crowd in life,
    'Mid the argumental tumult,
        Protestation, and endless strife;

    Mole-like burrowing in darkness,
        Grasping for the spider's thread,
    Always thwarted in ambition,
        Until the living join the dead?

—P-73

Americans

The Americans are a mighty people who never give up or get tired or sleep or dream. If these people hate someone, they will kill him by negligence, and if they like or love a person, they will shower him with affection.

—SP-ST-82

Ancestry

A man is not noble through ancestry;
How many noblemen are descendants of murderers?

—MS-74

Anthropomorphism

The mountains, trees, and rivers change their appearance with the vicissitudes of times and seasons, as a man changes with his experiences and emotions. The lofty poplar that resembles a bride in the daytime, will look like a column of smoke in the evening; the huge rock that stands impregnable at noon, will appear to be a miserable pauper at night, with earth for his bed and the sky for his cover; and the rivulet that we see glittering in the morning and hear singing the hymn of Eternity, will, in the evening, turn to a stream of tears wailing like a mother bereft of her child.

—BW-ST-78

Appearance

The appearance of things changes according to the emotions, and thus we see magic and beauty in them, while the magic and beauty are really in ourselves.

—BW-ST-51

The purpose of the spirit in the
Heart is concealed, and by outer
Appearance cannot be judged.

—T-372

Art

Art must be a direct communication between the artist's imagination and that of the looker. For that reason, I avoid, so much as possible, busying the looker's eye with too many details in order that his imagination may roam wide and far. As to the physical molds, art is forced to create for expressing itself; they must be beautiful molds. Otherwise, art defeats its purpose.

—KG-P-102

Is it really God that created Man, or is it the opposite? Imagination is the only creator, its nearest and clearest manifestation is Art; yes, art is life, life is art; all else is trite and empty in comparison.

—KG-P-97

Art is one step from the visibly known toward the unknown.

—MS-71

Artist

I should be a traitor to my art if I were to borrow my sitter's eyes. The face is a marvelous mirror that reflects most faithfully the innermost of the soul; the artist's business is to see that and portray it; otherwise he is not fit to be called an artist.

—KG-P-97

Authority

Selfishness, my brother, is the cause of blind superiority, and superiority creates clanship, and clanship creates authority which leads to discord and subjugation.

The soul believes in the power of knowledge and justice over dark ignorance; it denies the authority that supplies the swords to defend and strengthen ignorance and oppression—that authority which destroyed Babylon and shook the foundation of Jerusalem and left Rome in ruins. It is that which made people call criminals great men; made writers respect their names; made historians relate the stories of their inhumanity in manner of praise.

—TL-T-8

B

Barrenness

> How many flowers
> Possess no fragrance from the day
> Of their birth! How many clouds
> Gather in the sky, barren of rain,
> Dropping no pearls!

—T-373

Beauty

Beauty is that which attracts your soul, and that which loves to give and not receive. When you meet Beauty, you feel that the hands deep within your inner self are stretched forth to bring her into the domain of your heart. It is a magnificence combined of sorrow and joy; it is the Unseen which you see, and the Vague which you understand, and the Mute which you hear—it is the Holy of Holies that begins in yourself and ends vastly beyond your earthly imagination.

—TL-T-407

Are you troubled by the many faiths that Mankind professes? Are you lost in the valley of conflicting beliefs? Do you think that the freedom of heresy is less burdensome than the yoke of submission, and the liberty of dissent safer than the stronghold of acquiescence?

If such be the case, then make Beauty your religion, and worship her as your godhead; for she is the visible, manifest and perfect handiwork of God. Cast off those how have toyed with godliness as if it were a sham, joining together greed and arrogance; but believe instead in the divinity of beauty that is at once the beginning of your worship of Life, and the source of your hunger for Happiness.

Do penance before Beauty, and atone for your sins, for Beauty brings your heart closer to the throne of woman, who is the mirror of your affections and the teacher of your heart in the ways of Nature, which is your life's home.

—WM-ST-33

Only our spirits can understand beauty, or live and grow with it. It puzzles our minds; we are unable to describe it in words; it is a sensation that our eyes cannot see, derived from both the one who observes and the one who is looked upon. Real beauty is a ray which emanates from the holy of holies of the spirit, and illuminates the body, as life comes from the depths of the earth and gives color and scent to a flower.

—BW-ST-34

Beauty is that harmony between joy and sorrow which begins in our holy of holies and ends beyond the scope of our imagination.

—KG-P-93

Beauty is not in the face;
Beauty is a light in the heart.

—MS-75

Being

It is impossible for the mirror of the soul to reflect in the imagination anything which does not stand before it. It is impossible for the calm lake to show in its depth the figure of any mountain or the picture of any tree or cloud that does not exist close by the lake. It is impossible for the light to throw upon the earth a shadow of an object that has no being. Nothing can be seen, heard, or otherwise sensed unless it has actual *being*.

—SH-T-149

Believer

When you *know* a thing, you *believe* it, and the true believer sees with his *spiritual discernment* that which the surface investigator cannot see with the eyes of his head, and he understands through his *inner* thought that which the outside examiner cannot understand with his demanding, acquired process of thought.

The believer acquaints himself with the sacred realities through deep senses different from those used by others. A believer looks upon his senses as a great wall surrounding him, and when he walks upon the path he says, "This city has no exit, but it is perfect within." The believer lives for all the days and the nights and the unfaithful live but a few hours.

—SH-T-149

Body

He who endeavours to cleave the body from the spirit, or the spirit from the body is directing his heart away from truth. The flower and its fragrance are one, and the blind who deny the colour and the image of the flower, believing that it possesses only a fragrance vibrating the ether, are like those with pinched nostrils who believe that flowers are naught but pictures and colours, possessing no fragrance.

—SH-T-139

Life is naked. A nude body is the truest and noblest symbol of life. If I draw a mountain as a heap of human forms and paint a waterfall in the shape of tumbling human bodies, it is because I see in the mountain a heap of living things, and in the waterfall a precipitate current of life.

—KG-P-102

Boston
This city was called in the past the city of science and art, but today it is the city of traditions. The souls of its inhabitants are petrified; even their thoughts are old and worn-out. The strange thing about this city is that the petrified is always proud and boastful, and the worn-out and old holds its chin high.

—SP-ST-53

Bounty
An eternal hunger for love and beauty is my desire; I know now that those who possess bounty alone are naught but miserable, but to my spirit the sighs of lovers are more soothing than music of the lyre.

—T-413

Bravery
Bravery is a volcano; the seed of wavering does not grow on its crater.

—MS-72

Brotherhood

I love you because you are weak before the strong op-
pressor, and poor before the greedy rich. For these reasons I
shed tears and comfort you; and from behind my tears I see
you embraced in the arms of Justice, smiling and forgiving
your persecutors. You are my brother and I love you.

—TL-T-7

I love you, my brother, whoever you are—whether you
worship in your church, kneel in your temple, or pray in
your mosque. You and I are all children of one faith, for the
divers paths of religion are fingers of the loving hand of one
Supreme Being, a hand extended to all, offering complete-
ness of spirit to all, eager to receive all.

—WM-ST-69

C

Chains

Not everyone in chains is subdued;
At times, a chain is greater than a necklace.

—MS-74

Charity

The coin which you drop into
The withered hand stretching toward
You is the only golden chain that
Binds your rich heart to the
Loving heart of God. . . .

—SH-T-345

Chatter

I abstain from the people who consider insolence, bravery and tenderness cowardice. And I abstain from those
who consider chatter wisdom and silence ignorance.

—MS-71

Childhood

The things which the child loves remain in the domain of
the heart until old age. The most beautiful thing in life is

that our souls remain hovering over the places where we
once enjoyed ourselves.

—SP-ST-27

Churches

Oh Jesus, they have built these churches for the sake of
their own glory, and embellished them with silk and melted
gold. . . . They left the bodies of Thy chosen poor wrapped
in tattered raiment in the cold night. . . . They filled the sky
with the smoke of burning candles and incense and left the
bodies of Thy faithful worshippers empty of bread. . . .
They raised their voices with hymns of praise, but deafened
themselves to the cry and moan of the widows and orphans.

Come again, Oh Living Jesus, and drive the vendors of
Thy faith from Thy sacred temple, for they have turned it
into a dark cave where vipers of hypocrisy and falsehood
crawl and abound.

—SH-T-81

Citizenship

What is it to be a good citizen?

It is to acknowledge the other person's rights before as-
serting your own, but always to be conscious of your own.

It is to be free in word and deed, but it is also to know
that your freedom is subject to the other person's freedom.

It is to create the useful and the beautiful with your own
hands, and to admire what others have created in love and
with faith.

It is to produce by labor and only by labor and to spend
less than you have produced that your children may not be
dependent upon the state for support when you are no
more.

—MS-35

City

Oh people of the noisome city, who are living in darkness, hastening toward misery, preaching falsehood, and speaking with stupidity . . . until when shall you remain ignorant? Until when shall you abide in the filth of life and continue to desert its gardens? Why wear your tattered robes of narrowness while the silk raiment of Nature's beauty is fashioned for you? The lamp of wisdom is dimming; it is time to furnish it with oil. The house of true fortune is being destroyed; it is time to rebuild it and guard it. The thieves of ignorance have stolen the treasure of your peace; it is time to retake it!

—TL-T-403

Civilization

The misery of our Oriental nations is the misery of the world, and what you call *civilization* in the West is naught but another spectre of the many phantoms of tragic deception.

—SH-T-25

Inventions and discoveries are but amusement and comfort of the body when it is tired and weary. The conquest of distance and the victory over the seas are but false fruit which do not satisfy the soul, nor nourish the heart, neither lift the spirit, for they are afar from nature. And those structures and theories which man calls knowledge and art are naught except shackles and golden chains which man drags, and he rejoices with their glittering reflections and ringing sounds. They are strong cages whose bars man commenced fabricating ages ago, unaware that he was building from the inside, and that he would soon become his own prisoner to eternity.

—SH-T-26

Clergyman
The clergyman erects his temple upon the graves and bones of the devoted worshippers.

—SR-T-269

Concealment
Conceal your passion; your sickness is also your medicine because love to the soul is as wine in a glass—what you see is liquid, what is hidden is its spirit. . . .

Conceal your troubles; then, should the seas roar and the skies fall, you will be safe.

—MS-76

Conscience
Conscience is a just but weak judge. Weakness leaves it powerless to execute its judgment.

—TM-ST-118

Contentment
Be not satisfied with partial contentment, for he who engulfs the spring of life with one empty jar will depart with two full jars.

—SH-T-136

Fortune craves not Contentment, for it is an earthly hope, and its desires are embraced by union with objects, while Contentment is naught but heartfelt.

—TL-T-92

Contradiction
Contradiction is a lower degree of intelligence.

—MS-72

Counsel

My brothers, seek counsel of one another, for therein lies the way out of error and futile repentance. The wisdom of the many is your shield against tyranny. For when we turn to one another for counsel we reduce the number of our enemies.

—WM-ST-67

My soul is my counsel and has taught me to give ear to the voices which are created neither by tongues nor uttered by throats.

Before my soul became my counsel, I was dull, and weak of hearing, reflecting only upon the tumult and the cry. But, now, I can listen to silence with serenity and can hear in the silence the hymns of ages chanting exaltation to the sky and revealing the secrets of eternity.

—MS-V

Country Life

We who live amid the excitements of the city know nothing of the life of the mountain villagers. We are swept into the current of urban existence, until we forget the peaceful rhythms of simple country life, reap in autumn, rest in winter, imitating nature in all her cycles. We are wealthier than the villagers in silver or gold, but they are richer in spirit. What we sow we reap not; they reap what they sow. We are slaves of gain, and they the children of contentment. Our draught from the cup of life is mixed with bitterness and despair, fear and weariness; but they drink the pure nectar of life's fulfillment.

—TM-ST-53

Courage

The spirit who has seen the spectre of death cannot be scared by the faces of thieves; the soldier who has seen the swords glittering over his head and streams of blood under his feet does not care about rocks thrown at him by the children on the streets.

—BW-ST-106

Courser

My soul, living is like a courser of the night; the swifter its flight, the nearer the dawn.

—WM-ST-69

Creeds

People's creeds come forth, then perish
Like the shadows in the night.

—P-46

Criminal

For the Criminal who is weak and poor the
Narrow cell of death awaits; but
Honour and glory await the rich who
Conceal their crimes behind their
Gold and silver and inherited glory.

—T-364

D

Darkness

God has bestowed upon you intelligence and knowledge. Do not extinguish the lamp of Divine Grace and do not let the candle of wisdom die out in the darkness of lust and error. For a wise man approaches with his torch to light up the path of mankind.

—WM-ST-62

Death

Man is like the foam of the sea, that floats upon the surface of the water. When the wind blows, it vanishes, as if it had never been. Thus are our lives blown away by Death.

—WM-ST-31

The Reality of Life is Life itself, whose beginning is not in the womb, and whose ending is not in the grave. For the years that pass are naught but a moment in eternal life; and the world of matter and all in it is but a dream compared to the awakening which we call the terror of Death.

—WM-ST-32

The soul is an embryo in the body of
Man, and the day of death is the
Day of awakening, for it is the
Great era of labour and the rich
Hour of creation.

—T-373

Death is an ending to the son of
The earth, but to the soul it is
The start, the triumph of life.

—T-374

Death removes but the
Touch, and not the awareness of
All good. And he who has lived
One spring or more possesses the
Spiritual life of one who has
Lived a score of springs.

—T-375

A child in the womb, no sooner born than returned to the
earth—such is the fate of man, the fate of nations and of the
sun, the moon, and the stars.

—S

Despair
Despair is an ebb for every flow in the heart; it's a mute
affection.

—SP-ST-57

Despair weakens our sight and closes our ears. We can
see nothing but spectres of doom, and can hear only the
beating of our agitated hearts.

—BW-ST-98

Despot

The ignorant nations arrest their good men and turn them into their despots; and a country, ruled by a tyrant, persecutes those who try to free the people from the yoke of slavery.

—SR-T-274

Destiny

Man possesses a destiny
Which impels his thoughts and
Actions and words, and that not
Sufficing, directs his footsteps to
A place of unwilling abode.

—T-376

Destruction

I am indeed a fanatic and I am inclined toward destruction as well as construction. There is hatred in my heart for that which my detractors sanctify, and love for that which they reject. And if I could uproot certain customs, beliefs, and traditions of the people, I would do so without hesitation. When they said my books were poison, they were speaking truth about themselves, for what I say is poison to them. But they falsified when they said I mix honey into it, for I apply the poison full strength and pour it from transparent glass. Those who call me an idealist becalmed in clouds are the very ones who turn away from the transparent glass they call poison, knowing that their stomachs cannot digest it.

—TM-ST-91

Devil

Remember, one just man causes the Devil greater affliction than a million blind believers.

—WM-ST-62

Dichotomy

He who does not see the angels and devils in the beauty
and malice of life will be far removed from knowledge, and
his spirit will be empty of affection.

—BW-ST-20

Divinity

Remember that Divinity is the true self of Man. It cannot
be sold for gold; neither can it be heaped up as are the
riches of the world today. The rich man has cast off his
Divinity, and has clung to his gold. And the young today
have forsaken their Divinity and pursue self-indulgence
and pleasure.

—WM-ST-65

Doctors

Since the beginning of the world, the doctors have been
trying to save the people from their disorders; some used
knives, while others used potions, but pestilence spread
hopelessly. It is my wish that the patient would content
himself with remaining in his filthy bed, meditating his
long-continued sores; but instead, he stretches his hands
from under the robe and clutches at the neck of each who
comes to visit him, choking him to death. What irony it is!
The evil patient kills the doctor, and then closes his eyes
and says within himself, "He was a great physician."

—SH-T-23

E

Earth

The earth that opens wide her mouth to swallow man and his works is the redeemer of our souls from bondage to our bodies.

—WM-ST-79

East and West

The West is not higher than the East, nor is the West lower than the East, and the difference that stands between the two is not greater than the difference between the tiger and the lion. There is a just and perfect law that I have found behind the exterior of society, which equalizes misery, prosperity, and ignorance; it does not prefer one nation to another, nor does it oppress one tribe in order to enrich another.

—SH-T-25

Edifice

What man is capable of leaving an edifice on whose construction he has spent all his life, even though that edifice is his own prison? It is difficult to get rid of it in one day.

—SP-ST-83

Equality
One hour devoted to mourning and lamenting the
Stolen equality of the weak is nobler than a
Century filled with greed and usurpation.

—TL-T-412

Eternity
Each thing that exists remains forever, and the very existence of existence is proof of its eternity. But without that re-
alization, which is the knowledge of perfect being, man
would never know whether there was existence or nonexistence. If eternal existence is altered, then it must become
more beautiful; and if it disappears, it must return with
more sublime image; and if it sleeps, it must dream of a better awakening, for it is ever greater upon its rebirth.

—SH-T-143

Only those return to Eternity
Who on earth seek out Eternity.

—TL-T-410

Evolution
The law of evolution has a severe and oppressive countenance and those of limited or fearful mind dread it; but its
principles are just, and those who study them become en-
lightened. Through its Reason men are raised above themselves and can approach the sublime.

—TM-ST-99

Excess
In battling evil, excess is good; for he who is moderate in
announcing the truth is presenting half-truth. He conceals
the other half out of fear of the people's wrath.

—TM-ST-96

I will not be surprised if the "thinkers" say of me, "He is a man of excess who looks upon life's seamy side and reports nothing but gloom and lamentation."

—TM-ST-95

Exile
He who does not prefer exile to slavery is not free by any measure of freedom, truth and duty.

—SR-T-224

Eye
I feel pity toward those who admit of the eternity of the elements of which the eye is made, but at the same time doubt the eternity of the various objects of sight which employ the eye as a medium.

—SH-T-144

Man's eye is a magnifier; it shows him the earth much larger than it is.

—MS-71

F

Face

A look which reveals inward stress adds more beauty to the face, no matter how much tragedy and pain it bespeaks; but the face which, in silence, does not announce hidden mysteries is not beautiful, regardless of the symmetry of its features. The cup does not entice our lips unless the wine's color is seen through the transparent crystal.

—BW-ST-67

Faith

God has made many doors opening into truth which He opens to all who knock upon them with hands of faith.

—SH-T-138

Fame

There is something in our life which is nobler and more supreme than fame; and this *something* is the great deed that invokes fame.

—SP-ST-32

Fate

> Circumstances drive us on
>> In narrow paths by Kismet hewn.
>
> For Fate has ways we cannot change,
>> While weakness preys upon our Will;
> We bolster with excuse the self,
>> And help that Fate ourselves to kill.

—P-74

Life takes us up and bears us from one place to another; Fate moves us from one point to another. And we, caught up between these twain, hear dreadful voices and see only that which stands as a hindrance and obstacle in our path.

—WM-ST-46

Fear of Death

> Fear of death is a delusion
>> Harbored in the breast of sages;
> He who lives a single Springtime
>> Is like one who lives for ages.

—P-71

Fertility

> The body is a womb to soul
>> In which it dwells until full term,
> When it ascends once more to soar,
>> While womb again recedes to germ.

—P-67

First Love

Every young man remembers his first love and tries to recapture that strange hour, the memory of which changes his

deepest feeling and makes him so happy in spite of all the
bitterness of its mystery.

—BW-ST-12

Flowers

The flowers of the field are the children of sun's affection
and nature's love; and the children of men are the flowers
of love and compassion.

—BW-ST-122

Folly

The fool sees naught but folly; and the madman only
madness. Yesterday I asked a foolish man to count the fools
among us. He laughed and said, "This is too hard a thing to
do, and it will take too long. Were it not better to count only
the wise?"

—WM-ST-55

I once heard a learned man say, "Every evil has its rem-
edy, except folly. To reprimand an obstinate fool or to
preach to a dolt is like writing upon the water. Christ healed
the blind, the halt, the palsied, and the leprous. But the fool
He could not cure."

—WM-ST-56

Forbidden

When you behold a man turning aside from
Things forbidden that bring
Abysmal crime to self, look
Upon him with eyes of love, for
He is a preserver of God in him.

—T-372

Freedom

I love freedom, and my love for true
Freedom grew with my growing knowledge
Of the people's surrender to slavery
And oppression and tyranny, and of
Their submission to the horrible idols
Erected by the past ages and polished
By the parched lips of the slaves.
But I love those slaves with my love
For freedom, for they blindly kissed
The jaws of ferocious beasts in calm
And blissful unawareness, feeling not
The venom of the smiling vipers, and
Unknowingly digging their graves with
Their own fingers.

—SH-T-100

Dying for Freedom is nobler than living in
The shadow of weak submission, for
He who embraces death with the sword
Of Truth in his hand will eternalize
With the Eternity of Truth, for Life
Is weaker than Death and Death is
Weaker than Truth.

—SH-T-342

The free on earth builds of his strife
A prison for his own duress,
When he is freed from his own kin,
Is slave to thought and love's caress.

—P-55

Life without Freedom is like a body without a soul, and
Freedom without Thought is like a confused spirit. . . . Life,

Freedom, and Thought are three-in-one, and are everlasting
and never pass away.

—TM-ST-62

Freedom bids us to her table where we may partake of
her savory food and rich wine; but when we sit down at her
board, we eat ravenously and glut ourselves.

—WM-ST-47

You may chain my hands and shackle my feet; you may
even throw me into a dark prison, but you shall not enslave
my thinking because it is free.

—S

Friendship
Friendship with the ignorant is as foolish as arguing with
a drunkard.

—WM-ST-62

G

Gentleness

The gentleness of some is like
A polished shell with silky feel,
Lacking the precious pearl within
Oblivious of the brother's weal.

When you shall meet one who is strong
And gentle too, pray feast your eyes;
For he is glorious to behold,
The blind can see his qualities.

—P-59

Giants

We live in an era whose humblest men are becoming greater than the greatest men of preceding ages. What once preoccupied our minds is now of no consequence. The veil of indifference covers it. The beautiful dreams that once hovered in our consciousness have been dispersed like mist. In their place are giants moving like tempests, raging like seas, breathing like volcanoes.

What destiny will the giants bring the world at the end of their struggles? . . .

What will be the destiny of your country and mine? Which giant shall seize the mountains and valleys that produced us and reared us and made us men and women before the face of the sun? . . .

Which one of you people does not ponder day and night on the fate of the world under the rule of the giants intoxicated with the tears of widows and orphans?

—TM-ST-97

Glory

One hour devoted to the pursuit of Beauty
And Love is worth a full century of glory
Given by the frightened weak to the strong.

—TL-T-411

I have seen you, my brother, sitting upon the throne of glory, and around you stood your people acclaiming your majesty, and singing praises of your great deeds, extolling your wisdom, and gazing upon you as though in the presence of a prophet, their spirits exulting even to the canopy of heaven.

And as you gazed upon your subjects, I saw in your face the marks of happiness and power and triumph, as if you were the soul of their body.

But when I looked again, behold I found you alone in your loneliness, standing by the side of your throne, an exile stretching his hand in every direction, as if pleading for mercy and kindness from invisible ghosts—begging for shelter, even such as has naught in it but warmth and friendliness.

—WM-ST-42

God

Man has worshipped his own self since the beginning, calling that self by appropriate titles, until now, when he employs the word "God" to mean that same self.

—SH-T-391

Most religions speak of God in the masculine gender. To me He is as much a mother as He is a Father. He is both the father and the mother in one; and Woman is the God-Mother. The God-Father may be reached through the mind or the imagination. But the God-Mother can be reached through the heart only—through love. And Love is that holy wine which the gods distill from their hearts and pour into the hearts of men. Those only taste it pure and divine whose hearts have been cleansed of all the animal lusts. For clean hearts to be drunk with love is to be drunk with God. Those, on the other hand, who drink it mixed with the wines of earthly passions taste but the orgies of devils in Hell.

—KG-P-94

It were wiser to speak less of God, Whom we cannot understand, and more of each other, whom we may understand. Yet I would have you know that we are the breath and the fragrance of God. We are God, in leaf, in flower, and oftentimes in fruit.

—MS-43

Gold

Gold leads into gold, then into restlessness, and finally into crushing misery.

—TL-T-403

The life that the rich man spends in heaping up gold is in truth like the life of the worms in the grave. It is a sign of fear.

—WM-ST-65

Good

> The good in man should freely flow,
>   As evil lives beyond the grave;
> While Time with fingers moves the pawns
>   Awhile, then breaks the knight and knave.

—P-41

Governor

Are you a governor looking down on those you govern, never stirring abroad except to rifle their pockets or to exploit them for your own profit? If so, you are like tares about the threshing floor of the nation.

Are you a devoted servant who loves the people and is ever watchful over their welfare, and zealous for their success? If so, you are a blessing in the granaries of the land.

—WM-ST-35

H

Hands

How small is the life of the person who places his hands between his face and the world, seeing naught but the narrow lines of his hands!

—SH-T-150

Happiness

I sought happiness in my solitude, and
As I drew close to her I heard my soul
Whisper into my heart, saying, "The
Happiness you seek is a virgin, born
And reared in the depths of each heart,
And she emerges not from her birthplace."
And when I opened my heart to find her,
I discovered in its domain only her
Mirror and her cradle and her raiment,
And happiness was not there.

—SH-T-101

Happiness is a myth we seek,
If manifested surely irks;

Like river speeding to the plain,
   On its arrival slows and murks.

For man is happy only in
   His aspiration to the heights;
When he attains his goal, he cools
   And longs for other distant flights.

                                 —P-57

Happiness on earth is but a fleet,
Passing ghost, which man craves
At any cost in gold or time. And
When the phantom becomes the
Reality, man soon wearies of it.

                                 —T-371

Hardship

Braving obstacles and hardships is nobler than retreat to tranquility. The butterfly that hovers around the lamp until it dies is more admirable than the mole that lives in a dark tunnel.

                                 —BW-ST-89

Hate

I use hate as a weapon to defend myself; had I been strong, I would never have needed that kind of weapon.

                                 —MS-72

Heaven

The angels keep count of every tear shed by Sorrow; and they bring to the ears of the spirits hovering in the heavens of the Infinite each song of Joy wrought from our affections.

There, in the world to come, we shall see and feel all the vibrations of our feelings and the motions of our hearts. We shall understand the meaning of the divinity within us, whom we contemn because we are prompted by Despair.

—WM-ST-32

Hell

> Hell is not in torture;
> Hell is in an empty heart.

—MS-74

Herd

> Say not, "There goes a learned man"
>   Nor, "There a chieftain dignified."
> The best of men are in the herd,
>   And heed the shepherd as their guide.

—P-41

Honors

> Honors are but false delusions,
>   Like the froth upon the wave.
>
> Should the almond spray its blossoms
>   On the turf around its feet,
> Never will it claim a lordship,
>   Nor disdain the grass to greet.

—P-55

Hope

> Hope is found not in the forest,
>   Nor the wild portray despair;
> Why should forest long for portions
>   When the ALL is centered there?

Should one search the forest hopeful,
When *all nature* is the Aim?
For to hope is but an ailment,
So are station, wealth and fame.

—P-58

Humanity

Humanity is the spirit of the Supreme Being on earth, and that humanity is standing amidst ruins, hiding its nakedness behind tattered rags, shedding tears upon hollow cheeks, and calling for its children with pitiful voice. But the children are busy singing their clan's anthem; they are busy sharpening the swords and cannot hear the cry of their mothers.

Humanity is the spirit of the Supreme Being on earth, and the Supreme Being preaches love and good-will. But the people ridicule such teachings. The Nazarene Jesus listened, and crucifixion was his lot; Socrates heard the voice and followed it, and he too fell victim in body. The followers of The Nazarene and Socrates are the followers of Deity, and since people will not kill them, they deride them, saying, "Ridicule is more bitter than killing."

—TL-T-5

My soul preached to me and showed me that I am neither more than the pygmy, nor less than the giant.

Ere my soul preached to me, I looked upon humanity as two men: one weak, whom I pitied, and the other strong, whom I followed or resisted in defiance.

But now I have learned that I was as both are and made from the same elements. My origin is their origin, my conscience is their conscience, my contention is their contention, and my pilgrimage is their pilgrimage.

If they sin, I am also a sinner. If they do well, I take pride in their well-doing. If they rise, I rise with them. If they stay inert, I share their slothfulness.

—TM-ST-31

Hunger
A hungry man in a desert will not refuse to eat dry bread if Heaven does not shower him with manna and quails.

—BW-ST-40

Husband
Are you a husband who regards the wrongs he has committed as lawful, but those of his wife as unlawful? If so, you are like those extinct savages who lived in caves and covered their nakedness with hides.

Or are you a faithful companion, whose wife is ever at his side, sharing his every thought, rapture, and victory? If so, you are as one who at dawn walks at the head of a nation toward the high noon of justice, reason and wisdom.

—WM-ST-35

I

Ideas

How blind is the one who fancies and plans a matter in all true form and angles, and when he cannot prove it completely with superficial measurement and word proofs, believes that his idea and imagination were empty objects! But if he contemplates with sincerity and meditates upon these happenings, he will understand with conviction that his idea is as much a reality as is the bird of the sky, but that it is not yet crystallized, and that the idea is a segment of knowledge that cannot be proved with figures and words, for it is too high and too spacious to be imprisoned at that moment; too deeply imbedded in the spiritual to submit yet to the real.

—SH-T-148

Every beauty and greatness in this world is created by a single thought or emotion inside a man. Every thing we see today, made by past generations, was, before its appearance, a thought in the mind of a man or an impulse in the heart of a woman. The revolutions that shed so much blood and turned men's minds toward liberty were the idea of one man who lived in the midst of thousands of men. The devastating wars which destroyed empires were a thought that existed in the mind of an individual. The supreme teachings that changed the course of humanity were the ideas of a man whose genius separated him from his environment. A single thought built the Pyramids, founded the glory of Islam, and caused the burning of the library at Alexandria.

—BW-ST-49

Ignorance

In the house of Ignorance there is no mirror in which to view your soul.

—SH-T-87

During the ebb, I wrote a line upon the sand,
Committing to it all that is in my soul and mind;
I returned at the tide to read it and to ponder upon it,
I found naught upon the seashore but my ignorance.

—MS-39

Illness

I have found pleasure in being ill. This pleasure differs with its effect from any other pleasure. I have found a sort of tranquility that makes me love illness. The sick man is safe from people's strife, demands, dates and appointments . . . I have found another kind of enjoyment through illness which is more important and unmeasurable. I have found that I am closer to abstract things in my sickness than in health.

—SP-ST-84

I have pleasure in being ill. This pleasure differs with its effect from other pleasure. I have found a sort of tranquility that makes me love illness. The sick man is safe from people's strife, demands, dates and appointments, excess of talking and ringing of telephones. . . . I have found that I am closer to abstract things in my sickness than in health. When I lay my head and close my eyes and lose myself to the world, I find myself flying like a bird over serene valleys and forests, wrapped in a gentle veil. I see myself close to those whom my heart has loved, calling and talking to them, but without anger and with the same feelings they feel and the same thoughts they think. They lay their hands now and then upon my forehead to bless me.

—SP-P-34

Illusion

> Man's will is a floating shadow
> In the mind he conceives,
> And the rights of mankind pass and
> Perish like the Autumn leaves.

—P-51

Imagination

Thoughts have a higher dwelling place than the visible world, and its skies are not clouded by sensuality. Imagination finds a road to the realm of the gods, and there man can glimpse that which is to be after the soul's liberation from the world of substance.

—TM-ST-74

With one leap it (the imagination) would reach the core of life, divest it of all excrescences, then burn these excrescences and fling their ashes into the eyes of those who brought them into being. So must all imaginations be.

—KG-P-24

Imitation

> The people of the city feign great
> Wisdom and knowledge, but their
> Fancy remains false forever, for
> They are but experts of imitation.
> It gives them pride to calculate
> That a barter will bring no loss
> Or gain. The idiot imagines himself
> A king and no power can alter his
> Great thoughts and dreams. The
> Proud fool mistakes his mirror for
> The sky, and his shadow for a
> Moon that gleams high from the
> Heavens.

—T-368

Immortality

> Death on earth, to son of earth
>   Is final, but to him who is
> Ethereal, it is but the start
>   Of triumph certain to be his.
>
> If one embraces dawn in dreams,
>   He is immortal! Should he sleep
> His long night through, he surely fades
>   Into a sea of slumber deep.
>
> For he who closely hugs the ground
>   When wide awake will crawl 'til end.
> And death, like sea, who braves it light
>   Will cross it. Weighted will descend.

—P-70

If I did not covet immortality, I would never have learned the song which has been sung through all of time.

Rather, I would have been a suicide, nothing remaining of me except my ashes hidden within the tomb. . . .

Life is a darkness which ends as in the sunburst of the day.

The yearning of my heart tells me there is peace in the grave.

If some fool tells you the soul perishes like the body and that which dies never returns, tell him the flower perishes but the seed remains and lies before us as the secret of life everlasting.

—MS-58

Impermanence
> Mankind is like verses written
> Upon the surface of the rills.

—P-35

Indictment
I will gladly exchange my outcries for cheerful laughter, speak eulogies instead of indictments, replace excess with moderation, provided you show me a just governor, a lawyer of integrity, a religious hierarch who practices what he preaches, a husband who looks upon his wife with the same eyes as he looks upon himself.

—TM-ST-96

Infinite
We are naught but frail atoms in the heavens of the infinite; and we cannot but obey and surrender to the will of Providence.

If we love, our love is neither from us, nor is it for us. If we rejoice, our joy is not in us, but in Life itself. If we suffer,

our pain lies not in our wounds, but in the very heart of
Nature.

—WM-ST-23

Inheritance

The man who acquires his wealth by inheritance builds
his mansion with the weak poor's money.

—SR-T-269

Intoxication

The human turns to drugging,
As to nursing from the breast;
Coming to the age of weaning
Only when he's put to rest.

—P-39

Island

Life is an island in an ocean of loneliness, an island
whose rocks are hopes, whose trees are dreams, whose
flowers are solitude, and whose brooks are thirst.

Your life, my fellow men, is an island separated from all
other islands and regions. No matter how many are the
ships that leave your shores for other clinics, no matter how
many are the fleets that touch your coast, you remain a solitary island, suffering the pangs of loneliness and yearning
for happiness. You are unknown to your fellow men and far
removed from their sympathy and understanding.

—WM-ST-41

J

Jesus

Humanity looks upon Jesus the Nazarene as a poor-born Who suffered misery and humiliation with all of the weak. And He is pitied, for Humanity believes He was crucified painfully.... And all that Humanity offers to Him is crying and wailing and lamentation. For centuries Humanity has been worshipping weakness in the person of the Saviour.

The Nazarene was not weak! He was strong and is strong! But the people refuse to heed the true meaning of strength.

—SH-T-154

Jesus came not from the heart of the circle of Light to destroy the homes and build upon their ruins the convents and monasteries. He did not persuade the strong man to become a monk or a priest, but He came to send forth upon this earth a new spirit, with power to crumble the foundation of any monarchy built upon human bones and skulls ... He came to demolish the majestic palaces, constructed upon the graves of the weak, and crush the idols, erected upon the bodies of the poor. Jesus was not sent here to teach the people to build magnificent churches and temples amidst the cold wretched huts and dismal hovels. . . . He came to make the human heart a temple, and the soul an altar, and the mind a priest.

—SH-T-159

Surely you have prayed enough to last you to the end of your days, and hence forth you shall not enter a church as a worshipper; for the Jesus you love so dearly is not found in churches. Many are the places of worship, but few indeed are those who worship in Spirit and in truth.

—KG-P-19

Journalist

Are you a journalist who sells his principles in the markets of slaves and who fattens on gossip and misfortune and crime? If so, you are like a ravenous vulture preying upon rotting carrion.

—WM-ST-35

Judgment

The learned man who has not judgment is like an unarmed soldier proceeding into battle. His wrath will poison the pure spring of the life of his community and he will be like the grain of aloes in a pitcher of pure water.

—WM-ST-54

Justice

> Justice on earth would cause the Jinn
> To cry at misuse of the word,
> And were the dead to witness it,
> They'd mock at fairness in this world.

Yea, death and prison we mete out
  To small offenders of the laws,
While honor, wealth, and full respect
  On greater pirates we bestow.

To steal a flower we call mean,
  To rob a field is chivalry;
Who kills the body he must die,
  Who kills the spirit he goes free.

—P-47

What justice does authority display when it kills the killer? When it imprisons the robber? When it descends on a neighbouring country and slays its people? What does justice think of the authority under which a killer punishes the one who kills, and a thief sentences the one who steals?

—TL-T-9

When a man kills another man, the people says he is a murderer, but when the Emir kills him, the Emir is just. When a man robs a monastery, they say he is a thief, but when the Emir robs him of his life, the Emir is honourable. When a woman betrays her husband, they say she is an adulteress, but when the Emir makes her walk naked in the streets and stones her later, the Emir is noble. Shedding of blood is forbidden, but who made it lawful for the Emir? Stealing one's money is a crime, but taking away one's life is a noble act. Betrayal of a husband may be an ugly deed, but stoning of living souls is a beautiful sight. Shall we meet evil with evil and say this is the Law? Shall we fight corruption with greater corruption and say this is the Rule? Shall we conquer crimes with more crimes and say this is Justice?

—SR-T-315

The gifts which derive from justice are greater than those that spring from charity.

—WM-ST-65

K

Kin

He who understands you is greater kin to you than your own brother. For even your own kindred may neither understand you nor know your true worth.

—WM-ST-62

Kindness

From a sensitive woman's heart springs the happiness of mankind, and from the kindness of her noble spirit comes mankind's affection.

—ST-T-262

The kindness of the people is but an
Empty shell containing no gem or
Precious pearl. With two hearts do
People live; a small one of deep
Softness, the other of steel. And
Kindness is too often a shield,
And generosity too often a sword.

—T-367

Kingdom of Heaven

Vain are the beliefs and teachings that make man miserable, and false is the goodness that leads him into sorrow and despair, for it is man's purpose to be happy on this earth and lead the way to felicity and preach its gospel wherever he goes. He who does not see the kingdom of heaven in this life will never see it in the coming life. We came not into this life by exile, but we came as innocent creatures of God, to learn how to worship the holy and eternal spirit and seek the hidden secrets within ourselves from the beauty of life.

—SR-T-256

Kingdoms

Humans are divided into different clans and tribes, and belong to countries and towns. But I find myself a stranger to all communities and belong to no settlement. The universe is my country and the human family is my tribe.

Men are weak, and it is sad that they divide among themselves. The world is narrow and it is unwise to cleave it into kingdoms, empires, and provinces.

—TL-T-4

Knowledge

Learning follows various roads.
 We note the start but not the end.
For Time and Fate must rule the course,
 While we see not beyond the bend.

The best of knowledge is a dream
 The gainer holds steadfast, uncowed
By ridicule, and moves serene,
 Despised and lowly in the crowd.

—P-52

L

Law

What is Law? Who saw it coming with the sun from the depths of heaven? What human saw the heart of God and found its will or purpose? In what century did the angels walk among the people and preach to them, saying, "Forbid the weak from enjoying life, and kill the outlaws with the sharp edge of the sword, and step upon the sinners with iron feet"?

—SR-T-316

Are you a soldier compelled by the harsh law of man to forsake wife and children, and go forth into the field of battle for the sake of *Greed*, which your leaders mis-call *Duty*?

Are you a prisoner, pent up in a dark dungeon for some petty offense and condemned by those who seek to reform man by corrupting him?

Are you a young woman on whom God has bestowed beauty, but who has fallen prey to the base lust of the rich, who deceived you and bought your body but not your heart, and abandoned you to misery and distress?

If you are one of these, you are a martyr to man's law.

You are wretched, and your wretchedness is the fruit of the iniquity of the strong and the injustice of the tyrant, the brutality of the rich, and the selfishness of the lewd and the covetous.

—WM-ST-44

Man is weak by his own hand, for he
Has refashioned God's law into his own
Confining manner of life, chaining
Himself with the coarse irons of the
Rules of society which he desired; and
He is steadfast in refusing to be aware
Of the great tragedy he has cast upon
Himself and his children and their sons.
Man has erected on this earth a prison
Of quarrels from which he cannot now
Escape, and misery is his voluntary lot.

—T-366

Laws

People are saying that I am the enemy of just laws, of family ties and old tradition. Those people are telling the truth. I do not love man-made laws . . . I love the sacred and spiritual kindness which should be the source of every law upon the earth, for kindness is the shadow of God in man.

—MS-V

Human society has yielded for seventy centuries to corrupted laws until it cannot understand the meaning of superior and eternal laws. . . . Spiritual disease is inherited from one generation to another until it becomes a part of the people, who look upon it, not as a disease, but as a natural gift, showered by God on Adam. If these people found someone free from the germs of this disease, they would think of him with shame and disgrace.

—SP-P-31

Learning

Learning nourishes the seed but it gives you no seed of its own.

—MS-72

Reason and learning are like body and soul. Without the body, the soul is nothing but empty wind. Without the soul, the body is but a senseless frame.

Reason without learning is like the untilled soil, or like the human body that lacks nourishment.

—WM-ST-55

Learning is the only wealth tyrants cannot despoil. Only death can dim the lamp of knowledge that is within you. The true wealth of a nation lies not in its gold or silver but in its learning, wisdom, and in the uprightness of its sons.

—WM-ST-61

Liars

There are among the people murderers who have never committed murder, thieves who have never stolen and liars who have spoken nothing but the truth.

—MS-72

Liberty

I walked lonely in the Valley of the Shadow of Life, where the past attempts to conceal itself in guilt, and the soul of the future folds and rests itself too long. There, at the edge of Blood and Tears River, which crawled like a poisonous viper and twisted like a criminal's dreams, I listened to the frightened whisper of the ghosts of slaves, and gazed at nothingness.

When midnight came and the spirits emerged from hidden places, I saw a cadaverous, dying spectre fall to her knees, gazing at the moon. I approached her, asking, "What is your name?"

"My name is Liberty," replied this ghastly shadow of a corpse.

And I inquired, "Where are your children?"

And Liberty, tearful and weak, gasped, "One died crucified, another died mad, and the third one is not yet born."

She limped away and spoke further, but the mist in my eyes and cries of my heart prevented sight or hearing.

—SH-T-66

Everything on earth lives according to the law of nature, and from that law emerges the glory and joy of liberty; but man is denied this fortune, because he set for the God-given soul a limited and earthly law of his own. He made for himself strict rules. Man built a narrow and painful prison in which he secluded his affections and desires. He dug out a deep grave in which he buried his heart and its purpose. If an individual, through the dictates of his soul, declares his withdrawal from society and violates the law, his fellow-men will say he is a rebel worthy of exile, or an infamous creature worthy only of execution. Will man remain a slave of self-confinement until the end of the world? Or will he be freed by the passing of time and live in the Spirit for the Spirit? Will man insist upon staring downward and backward at the earth? Or will he turn his eyes toward the sun so he will not see the shadow of his body amongst the skulls and thorns?

—SR-T-228

Life

Man struggles to find life outside himself, unaware that the life he is seeking is within him.

—SH-T-144

Life is a woman bathing in the tears of her lovers and anointing herself with the blood of her victims. Her raiments are white days, lined with the darkness of night. She takes the human heart to lover, but denies herself in marriage.

> *Life is an enchantress*
> *Who seduces us with her beauty—*
> *But he who knows her wiles*
> *Will flee her enchantments.*

—WM-ST-85

How often I talked with Harvard professors, yet felt as if I were talking to a professor from Al-Azhar! How often I have conversed with some Bostonian ladies and heard them say things I used to hear from simple and ignorant old women in Syria! Life is one, Mikhail; it manifests itself in the villages of Lebanon as in Boston, New York, and San Francisco.

—KG-P-37

Light

The true light is that which emanates from within man, and reveals the secrets of the heart to the soul, making it happy and contented with life.

—SR-T-255

Limitation

The person who is limited in heart and thought is inclined to love that which is limited in life, and the weak-sighted cannot see more than one cubit ahead upon the path he treads, nor more than one cubit of the wall upon which he rests his shoulder.

—SH-T-129

Longing

In the will of man there is a power of longing which turns the mist in ourselves into sun.

—SP-ST-86

Love

The power to
Love is God's greatest gift to man,
For it never will be taken from the
Blessed one who loves.

—SH-T-99

Love lies in the soul alone,
Not in the body, and like wine
Should stimulate our better self
To welcome gifts of Love Divine.

—P-61

Man cannot reap love until after sad and revealing separation, and bitter patience, and desperate hardship.

—TL-T-115

Yesterday I stood at the temple door interrogating the passers-by about the mystery and merit of Love.

And before me passed an old man with an emaciated and melancholy face, who sighed and said:

"Love is a natural weakness bestowed upon us by the first man."

But a virile youth retorted:

"Love joins our present with the past and the future."

Then a woman with a tragic face sighed and said:

"Love is a deadly poison injected by black vipers, that crawl from the caves of hell. The poison seems fresh as dew and the thirsty soul eagerly drinks it; but after the first intoxication the drinker sickens and dies a slow death."

Then a beautiful, rosy-cheeked damsel smilingly said:

"Love is wine served by the brides of Dawn which strengthens strong souls and enables them to ascend to the stars."

After her a black-robed, bearded man, frowning, said:

"Love is the blind ignorance with which youth begins and ends."

Another, smiling, declared:

"Love is a divine knowledge that enables men to see as much as the gods."

Then a blind man, feeling his way with a cane:

"Love is a blinding mist that keeps the soul from discerning the secret of existence, so that the heart sees only trembling phantoms of desire among the hills, and hears only echoes of cries from voiceless valleys."

And a feeble ancient, dragging his feet like two rags, said, in quavering tones:

"Love is the rest of the body in the quiet of the grave, the tranquility of the soul in the depth of Eternity."

And a five-year-old child, after him, said laughing:

"Love is my father and mother, and no one knows Love save my father and mother."

And so, all who passed spoke of Love as the image of their hopes and frustrations, leaving it a mystery as before.

—TM-ST-88

Those whom Love has not chosen as followers do not hear when Love calls.

—BW-ST-75

Love is the only flower that grows and blossoms without the aid of seasons.

—BW-ST-54

Love is the only freedom in the world because it so elevates the spirit that the laws of humanity and the phenomena of nature do not alter its course.

—BW-ST-35

Love passes by us, robed in meekness; but we flee from her in fear, or hide in the darkness; or else pursue her, to do evil in her name.

—WM-ST-46

Love that comes between the naivete and awakening of youth satisfies itself with possessing, and grows with embraces. But Love which is born in the firmament's lap and has descended with the night's secrets is not contented with anything but Eternity and immortality; it does not stand reverently before anything except deity.

—BW-ST-114

If humanity were to
Lead love's cavalcade to a bed of
Faithless motive, then love there
Would decline to abide. Love is a
Beautiful bird, begging capture,
But refusing injury.

—T-369

Love,
When sought out, is an ailment
Between the flesh and the bone,
And only when youth has passed
Does the pain bring rich and
Sorrowful knowledge.

—T-369

Darkness may hide the trees and the flowers from the eyes but it cannot hide love from the soul.

—S

Lust

Beauty reveals herself to us as she sits on the throne of glory; but we approach her in the name of Lust, snatch off her crown of purity, and pollute her garment with our evil-doing.

—WM-ST-46

M

Madness

Madness is the first step towards unselfishness. Be mad and tell us what is behind the veil of "sanity." The purpose of life is to bring us closer to those secrets, and madness is the only means.

—SP-ST-62

Maiden

There is no affection purer and more soothing to the spirit than the one hidden in the heart of a maiden who awakens suddenly and fills her own spirit with heavenly music that makes her days like poets' dreams and her nights prophetic.

—SR-T-264

Mankind

I love mankind and I love equally all
Three human kinds . . . the one who
Blasphemes life, the one who blesses
It, and the one who meditates upon it.
I love the first for his misery and

The second for his generosity and the
Third for his perception and peace.

—SH-T-101

Marriage

Marriage is the union of two divinities that a third might
be born on earth. It is the union of two souls in a strong love
for the abolishment of separateness. It is that higher unity
which fuses the separate unities within the two spirits. It is
the golden ring in a chain whose beginning is a glance, and
whose ending is Eternity. It is the pure rain that falls from
an unblemished sky to fructify and bless the fields of divine
Nature.

—WM-ST-50

Merchant

Are you a merchant, drawing advantage from the needs
of the people, engrossing goods so as to resell them at an ex-
orbitant price? If so, you are a reprobate; and it matters
naught whether your home is a palace or a prison.

Or you are an honest man, who enables farmer and
weaver to exchange their products, who mediates between
buyer and seller, and through his just ways profits both
himself and others?

If so, you are a righteous man; and it matters not whether
you are praised or blamed.

—WM-ST-34

Mercy

Do not be merciful, but be just, for mercy is bestowed
upon the guilty criminal, while justice is all that an innocent
man requires.

—SR-T-276

Merriment

> Life is not only a merriment;
> Life is desire and determination.

—MS-74

Middle East

There are in the Middle East today two challenging ideas: old and new.

The old ideas will vanish because they are weak and exhausted.

There is in the Middle East an awakening that defies slumber. This awakening will conquer because the sun is its leader and the dawn is its army. . . .

There is on the horizon of the Middle East a new awakening; it is growing and expanding; it is reaching and engulfing all sensitive, intelligent souls; it is penetrating and gaining the sympathy of noble hearts.

The Middle East, today, has two masters. One is deciding, ordering, being obeyed; but he is at the point of death.

But the other one is silent in his conformity to law and order, calmly awaiting justice; he is a powerful giant who knows his own strength, confident in his existence and a believer in his destiny.

—MS-60

Mimic

He who repeats what he does not understand is no better than an ass that is loaded with books.

—WM-ST-63

Modern Generation

This strange generation exists between sleeping and waking. It holds in its hands the soil of the past and the seeds of the future.

—BW-ST-84

Modern Poetry

Oh spirits of the poets, who watch over us from the heaven of Eternity, we go to the altars you have adorned with the pearls of your thoughts and the gems of your souls because we are oppressed by the clang of steel and the clamor of factories. Therefore our poems are as heavy as freight trains and as annoying as steam whistles.

And you, the real poets, forgive us. We belong in the New World where men run after worldly goods; and poetry, too, is a commodity today, and not a breath of immortality.

—TM-ST-83

Modern Woman

Modern civilization has made woman a little wiser, but it has increased her suffering because of man's covetousness. The woman of yesterday was a happy wife, but the woman of today is a miserable mistress. In the past she walked blindly in the light, but now she walks open-eyed in the dark. She was beautiful in her ignorance, virtuous in her simplicity, and strong in her weakness. Today she has become ugly in her ingenuity, superficial and heartless in her knowledge. Will the day ever come when beauty and knowledge, ingenuity and virtue, and weakness of body and strength of spirit will be united in a woman?

—BW-ST-83

Modesty

To be modest in speaking truth is hypocrisy.

—TM-ST-95

Money

Money! The source of insincere love; the spring of false light and fortune; the well of poisoned water; the desperation of old age!

—TL-T-175

Money is a like a stringed instrument; he who does not know how to use it properly will hear only discordant music. Money is like love; it kills slowly and painfully the one who withholds it, and it enlivens the other who turns it upon his fellow men.

—TL-T-404

Mother

The mother is everything—she is our consolation in sorrow, our hope in misery, and our strength in weakness. She is the source of love, mercy, sympathy, and forgiveness. He who loses his mother loses a pure soul who blesses and guards him constantly.

Every thing in nature bespeaks the mother. The sun is the mother of earth and gives it its nourishment of heat; it never leaves the universe at night until it has put the earth to sleep to the song of the sea and the hymn of birds and brooks. And this earth is the mother of trees and flowers. It produces them, nurses them, and weans them. The trees and flowers become kind mothers of their great fruits and seeds. And the mother, the prototype of all existence, is the eternal spirit, full of beauty and love.

—BW-ST-92

Music

When God created Man, he gave him Music as a language different from all other languages. And early man sang her glory in the wilderness; and she drew the hearts of kings and moved them from their thrones.

—WM-ST-58

> The moaning flute is more divine
> Than the golden cup of deep, red wine.

—T-368

God created music as a common language for all men. It inspires the poets, the composers and the architects. It lures us to search our souls for the meaning of the mysteries described in ancient books.

—S

N

Nature

In the wild there is no Credo
Nor a hideous disbelief;
Song-birds never are assertive
Of the Truth, the Bliss, or Grief.

—P-46

When I began to draw and paint, I did not say to myself, "Behold Kahlil Gibran. There are ahead of you so many ways to art: The classic, the modern, the symbolistic, the impressionistic, and others. Choose for yourself one of them." I did nothing of the sort. I simply found my pen and brush, quite of themselves, recording symbols of my thoughts, emotions, and fancies. Some think the business of art to be a mere imitation of nature. But Nature is far too great and too subtle to be successfully imitated. No artist can ever reproduce even the least of Nature's surpassing creations and miracles. Besides, what profit is there in imitating Nature when she is so open and so accessible to all who see and hear? The business of art is rather to understand Nature and to reveal her meanings to those unable to understand. It is to convey the soul of a tree rather than to produce a fruitful likeness of the tree. It is to reveal the conscience of the sea, not to portray so many foaming waves or so much blue water. The mission of art is to bring out the unfamiliar from the most familiar.

Pity the eye that sees no more in the sun than a stove to keep it warm and a torch to light its way between the home and the business office. That is a blind eye, even if capable of seeing a fly a mile away. Pity the ear that hears no more than so many notes in the song of the nightingale. It is a deaf ear, even if capable of hearing the crawling of ants in their subterranean labyrinths.

—KG-P-100

Nature reaches out to us with welcoming arms, and bids us enjoy her beauty; but we dread her silence and rush into the crowded cities, there to huddle like sheep fleeing from a ferocious wolf.

—WM-ST-47

To Nature all are alive and all are
Free. The earthly glory of man is an
Empty dream, vanishing with the bubbles
In the rocky stream.

—T-367

Nature and Man

I heard the brook lamenting like a widow mourning her dead child and I asked, "Why do you weep, my pure brook?"

And the brook replied, "Because I am compelled to go to the city where Man contemns me and spurns me for stronger drinks and makes of me a scavenger for his offal, pollutes my purity, and turns my goodness to filth."

And I heard the birds grieving, and I asked, "Why do

available September 15

The Lost Symbol
by Dan Brown
author of The Da Vinci Code

40% OFF list price
reserve your copy today

STORE: 0225   REG: 03/17   TRAN#: 0079
SALE   08/14/2009   EMP: 02128

Periodicals, newspapers, comic books, food and drink, digital downloads, gift cards, return gift cards, items marked "non-returnable," "final sale" or the like and out-of-print, collectible or pre-owned items cannot be returned or exchanged.

Returns and exchanges to a Borders, Borders Express or Waldenbooks retail store of merchandise purchased from Borders.com may be permitted in certain circumstances. See Borders.com for details.

Returns

Returns of merchandise purchased from a Borders, Borders Express or Waldenbooks retail store will be permitted only if presented in saleable condition accompanied by the original sales receipt or Borders gift receipt within the time periods specified below. Returns accompanied by the original sales receipt must be made within 30 days of purchase and the purchase price will be refunded in the same form as the original purchase. Returns accompanied by the original Borders gift receipt must be made within 60 days of purchase and the you cry, my beautiful birds?" And one of them flew near, and perched at the tip of a branch and said, "The sons of Adam will soon come into this field with their deadly weapons and make war upon us as if we were their mortal enemies. We are now taking leave of one another, for we know not which of us will escape the wrath of Man. Death follows us wherever we go."

Now the sun rose from behind the mountain peaks, and gilded the treetops with coronals. I looked upon this beauty and asked myself, "Why must Man destroy what Nature has built?"

—WM-ST-83

Neighbor
When you tell your trouble to your neighbor you present him with a part of your heart. If he possesses a great soul, he thanks you; if he possesses a small one, he belittles you.

—MS-71

New York
He who wishes to live in New York must be a sharp sword in a sheath of honey. The sword is to repel those who are desirous of killing time, and the honey is to satisfy their hunger.

—SP-ST-83

Nightingale
The nightingale does not make his nest in a cage lest slavery be the lot of its chicks.

—BW-ST-122

O

Old Age

An old man likes to return in memory to the days of his youth like a stranger who longs to go back to his own country. He delights to tell stories of the past like a poet who takes pleasure in reciting his best poem. He lives spiritually in the past because the present passes swiftly, and the future seems to him an approach to the oblivion of the grave.

—BW-ST-24

Many are the men who curse with venom the dead days of their youth; many are the women who execrate their wasted years with the fury of the lioness who has lost her cubs; and many are the youths and maidens who are using their hearts only to sheath the daggers of the bitter memories of the future, wounding themselves through ignorance with the sharp and poisoned arrows of seclusion from happiness.

Old age is the snow of the earth; it must, through light and truth, give warmth to the seeds of youth below, protecting them and fulfilling their purpose.

—T-302

Oneness

All things in this creation exist within you, and all things in you exist in creation; there is no border between you and the closest things, and there is no distance between you and the farthest things, and all things, from the lowest to the loftiest, from the smallest to the greatest, are within you as equal things. In one atom are found all the elements of the earth; in one motion of the mind are found the motions of all the laws of existence; in one drop of water are found the secrets of all the endless oceans; in one aspect of *you* are found all the aspects of *existence*.

—SH-T-140

Opportunity

He who tries to seize an opportunity after it has passed him by is like one who sees it approach but will not go to meet it.

—WM-ST-56

Oppression

Woe to the nation that receives her conquerors beating the drums. Woe to the nation that hates oppression in her sleep and accepts it in her awakening. Woe to the nation that raises her voice only behind a coffin and prides itself only in the cemetery. Woe to a nation that does not revolt until her neck is placed on the scaffold.

—MS-99

Orient

The people of the Orient demand that the writer be like a bee always making honey. They are gluttonous for honey and prefer it to all other food.

The people of the Orient want their poet to burn himself as incense before their sultans. The Eastern skies have become sickly with incense yet the people of the Orient have had not enough. . . .

Numerous are the social healers in the Orient, and many are their patients who remain uncured but appear eased of their ills because they are under the effects of social narcotics. But these tranquilizers merely mask the symptoms.

Such narcotics are distilled from many sources but the chief is the Oriental philosophy of submission to Destiny (the act of God).

—TM-ST-92

P

Pacifism

Beware of the leader who says, "Love of existence obliges us to deprive the people of their rights!" I say unto you but this: protecting others' rights is the noblest and most beautiful human act; if my existence requires that I kill others, then death is more honourable to me, and if I cannot find someone to kill me for the protection of my honour, I will not hesitate to take my life by my own hands for the sake of Eternity before Eternity comes.

—TL-T-8

Pain

Pain is an unseen and powerful hand that breaks the skin of the stone in order to extract the pulp.

—SP-ST-94

Past and Future

I tell you that the children of yesteryears are walking in the funeral of the era that they created for themselves. They are pulling a rotted rope that might break soon and cause them to drop into a forgotten abyss. I say that they are living in homes with weak foundations; as the storm blows—

and it is about to blow—their homes will fall upon their heads and thus become their tombs. I say that all their thoughts, their sayings, their quarrels, their compositions, their books and all their work are nothing but chains dragging them because they are too weak to pull the load.

But the children of tomorrow are the ones called by life, and they follow it with steady steps and heads high, they are the dawn of new frontiers, no smoke will veil their eyes and no jingle of chains will drown out their voices. They are few in number, but the difference is as between a grain of wheat and a stack of hay. No one knows them but they know each other. They are like summits, which can see and hear each other—not like caves, which cannot hear or see. They are the seed dropped by the hand of God in the field, breaking through its pod and waving its sapling leaves before the face of the sun. It shall grow into a mighty tree, its root in the heart of the earth and its branches high in the sky.

—MS-64-65

Patriot

Are you a politician who says to himself: "I will use my country for my own benefit"? If so, you are naught but a parasite living on the flesh of others. Or are you a devoted patriot, who whispers into the ear of his inner self: "I love to serve my country as a faithful servant." If so, you are an oasis in the desert, ready to quench the thirst of the wayfarer.

—WM-ST-34

Patriotism

What is this duty that separates the lovers, and causes the women to become widows, and the children to become orphans? What is this patriotism which provokes wars and destroys kingdoms through trifles? And what cause can be more than trifling when compared to but one life? What is this duty which invites poor villagers, who are looked upon as nothing by the strong and by the sons of the inherited nobility, to die for the glory of their oppressors? If duty destroys peace among nations, and patriotism disturbs the tranquility of man's life, then let us say, "Peace be with duty and patriotism."

—SH-T-379

I have a yearning for my beautiful country, and I love its people because of their misery. But if my people rose, stimulated by plunder and motivated by what they call "patriotic spirit" to murder, and invaded my neighbour's country, then upon the committing of any human atrocity I would hate my people and my country.

—TL-T-4

Peace

Will peace be on earth while the sons of misery are slaving in the fields to feed the strong and fill the stomachs of the tyrants? Will ever peace come and save them from the clutches of destitution?

What is peace? Is it in the eyes of those infants, nursing upon the dry breasts of their hungry mothers in cold huts? Or is it in the wretched hovels of the hungry who sleep upon hard beds and crave for one bite of the food which the priests and monks feed to their fat pigs?

—SH-T-82

Perpetuity

I am saddened by the one who gazes upon the mountains and plains upon which the sun throws its rays, and who listens to the breeze singing the song of the thin

branches, and who inhales the fragrance of the flowers and
the jasmine, and then says within himself, "No . . . what I
see and hear will pass away, and what I know and feel will
vanish." This humble soul who sees and contemplates reverently the joys and sorrows about him, and then denies the
perpetuity of their existence, must himself vanish like
vapour in the air and disappear, for he is seeking darkness
and placing his back to truth. Verily, he is a living soul
denying *his* very existence, for he denies *other* of God's existing things.

—SH-T-144

Perplexity

Perplexity is the beginning of knowledge.

—WM-ST-87

Persecution

Persecution cannot harm him who stands by Truth. Did
not Socrates fall proudly a victim in body? Was not Paul
stoned for the sake of the Truth? It is our inner self that
hurts us when we disobey and kills us when we betray.

—SH-T-77

Philosophy

There is a desire deep within the soul which drives man
from the seen to the unseen, to philosophy and to the divine.

—MS-49

Pilgrimage

For every seed that autumn drops into the heart of the
earth, there exists a different manner of splitting the shell
from the pulp; then are created the leaves and then the
flowers, and then the fruit. But regardless of the fashion in

which this takes place, those plants must undertake one
sole pilgrimage, and their great mission is to stand before
the face of the sun.

—ST-T-141

Poet

Poet, you are the life of this life, and you have
Triumphed over the ages despite their severity.

Poet, you will one day rule the hearts, and
Therefore, your kingdom has no ending.

Poet, examine your crown of thorns; you will
Find concealed in it a budding wreath of laurel.

—TL-T-301

Are you a poet full of noise and empty sounds? If so, you
are like one of those mountebanks that make us laugh when
they are weeping, and make us weep, when they laugh.
Or are you one of those gifted souls in whose hands God
has placed a viola to soothe the spirit with heavenly music,
and bring his fellow men close to Life and the Beauty of
Life? If so, you are a torch to light us on our way, a sweet
longing in our hearts, and a revelation of the divine in our
dreams.

—WM-ST-36

Poets are unhappy people, for, no matter how high their
spirits reach, they will still be enclosed in an envelope of
tears.

—BW-ST-41

Poetry

Poetry, my dear friends, is a sacred incarnation of a smile. Poetry is a sigh that dries the tears. Poetry is a spirit who dwells in the soul, whose nourishment is the heart, whose wine is affection. Poetry that comes not in this form is a false messiah.

—TM-ST-83

If the spirits of Homer, Virgil, Al-Maary, and Milton had known that poetry would become a lapdog of the rich, they would have forsaken a world in which this could occur.

—TM-ST-82

Poor

Not all the poor are scorned;
The wealth of the world is in a loaf of bread and a cloak.

—MS-75

Popular Knowledge

Present knowledge of the people
Is a fog above the field;
When the sun mounts the horizon
To its rays the mist will yield.

—P-54

Position

Greatness is not in exalted position;
Greatness is for he who refuses position.

—MS-74

Possessiveness

Limited love asks for possession of the beloved, but the unlimited asks only for itself.

—BW-ST-114

Poverty

My fellow poor, Poverty sets off the nobility of the spirit, while wealth discloses its evil. Sorrow softens the feelings, and Joy heals the wounded heart. Were Sorrow and Poverty abolished, the spirit of man would be like an empty tablet, with naught inscribed save the signs of selfishness and greed.

—WM-ST-65

My poor friend, if you only knew that the Poverty which causes you so much wretchedness is the very thing that reveals the knowledge of Justice and the understanding of Life, you would be contented with your lot.

I say knowledge of Justice: for the rich man is too busy amassing wealth to seek this knowledge.

And I say understanding of Life: for the strong man is too eager in his pursuit of power and glory to keep to the straight path of truth.

Rejoice then, my poor friend, for you are the mouth of Justice and the book of Life. Be content, for you are the source of virtue in those who rule over you and the pillar of integrity of those who guide you.

—WM-ST-64

Praise

My soul preached to me and said, "Do not be delighted because of praise, and do not be distressed because of blame."

Ere my soul counseled me, I doubted the worth of my work.

Now I realize that the trees blossom in Spring and bear fruit in Summer without seeking praise; and they drop their leaves in Autumn and become naked in Winter without fearing blame.

—TM-ST-31

Prayer

Prayer is the song of the heart. It reaches the ear of God even if it is mingled with the cry and the tumult of a thousand men.

—S

Preaching

How painful is the preaching of the fortunate to the heart of the miserable! And how severe is the strong when he stands as advisor among the weak!

—SH-T-381

Priest

The priest is a traitor who uses the Gospel as a threat to ransom your money . . . a hypocrite wearing a cross and using it as a sword to cut your veins . . . a wolf disguised in lambskin . . . a glutton who respects the tables more than the altars . . . A gold hungry creature who follows the Dinar to the farthest land . . . a cheat pilfering from widows and orphans. He is a queer being, with an eagle's beak, a tiger's clutches, a hyena's teeth and a viper's clothes. Take the Book away from him and tear his raiment off and pluck his beard and do whatever you wish unto him; then place in his hand one Dinar, and he will forgive you smilingly.

—SR-T-281

When a villager doubts the holiness of the priest, he will be told, "Listen only to his teaching and disregard his shortcomings and misdeeds."

—TM-ST-94

Progress

Progress is not merely improving the past; it is moving forward toward the future.

—MS-71

Prophet

      The Prophet arrives
        Veiled in the cloak of future thought,
   'Mid people hid in ancient garb,
        Who could not see the gift he brought.

      He is a stranger to this life,
        Stranger to those who praise or blame,
   For he upholds the Torch of Truth,
        Although devoured by the flame.

—P-52

R

Reason
When Reason speaks to you, hearken to what she says, and you shall be saved. Make good use of her utterances, and you shall be as one armed. For the Lord has given you no better guide than Reason, no stronger arm than Reason. When Reason speaks to your inmost self, you are proof against Desire. For Reason is a prudent minister, a loyal guide, and a wise counsellor. Reason is light in darkness, as anger is darkness amidst light. Be wise—let Reason, not Impulse, be your guide.

—WM-ST-54

Rebellion
Life without Rebellion is like seasons without Spring. And Rebellion without Right is like Spring in an arid desert. . . . Life, Rebellion, and Right are three-in-one who cannot be changed or separated.

—TM-ST-62

Did God give us the breath of life to place it under death's feet? Did He give us liberty to make it a shadow for slavery? He who extinguishes his spirit's fire with his own hands is an infidel in the eyes of Heaven, for Heaven set the fire that burns in our spirits. He who does not rebel against oppression is doing himself injustice.

—BW-ST-112

Regret

Be not like him who sits by his fireside and watches the fire go out, then blows vainly upon the dead ashes. Do not give up hope or yield to despair because of that which is past, for to bewail the irretrievable is the worst of human frailties.

—WM-ST-68

Religion

If we were to do away with the various religions, we would find ourselves united and enjoying one great faith and religion, abounding in brotherhood.

—SH-T-135

Religion is a well-tilled field,
　　Planted and watered by desire
Of one who longed for Paradise,
　　Or one who dreaded Hell and Fire.

Aye, were it but for reckoning
　　At Resurrection, they had not
Worshipped God, nor did repent,
　　Except to gain a better lot—

As though religion were a phase
　　Of commerce in their daily trade;
Should they neglect it they would lose—
　　Or persevering would be paid.

—P-44

Religion to man is like a field,
For it is planted with hope and
Tended by the shivering ignorant,
Fearing the fire of hell; or it is
Sowed by the strong in wealth of
Empty gold who look upon religion
As a kind of barter, ever seeking
Profit in earthly reward. But
Their hearts are lost despite
Their throbbing, and the product
Of their spiritual farming is but
The unwanted weed of the valley.

—T-364

Religious Leader

Are you a leader of religion, who weaves out of the simplicity of the faithful a scarlet robe for his body; and of their kindness a golden crown for his head; and while living on Satan's plenty, spews forth his hatred of Satan? If so, you are a heretic; and it matters not that you fast all day and pray all night.

Or are you the faithful one who finds in the goodness of people a groundwork for the betterment of the whole nation; and in whose soul is the ladder of perfection leading to the Holy Spirit? If you are such, you are like a lily in the garden of Truth; and it matters not if your fragrance is lost upon men, or dispersed into the air, where it will be eternally preserved.

—WM-ST-34

Repentance

Paradise is not in repentance;
Paradise is in the pure heart.

—MS-74

Riches

Riches are not in money alone;
How many wanderers were the richest of all men?

—MS-75

Ruler

Between the frown of the tiger and the smile of the wolf
the flock is perished; the ruler claims himself as king of the
law, and the priest as the representative of God, and between these two, the bodies are destroyed and the souls
wither into nothing.

—SR-T-269

S

Sanity

> Eagles never display wonder,
> Or say, " 'Tis marvel of the age."
> For in nature we the children
> Only hold the sane as strange.

—P-64

Science

All around me are dwarves who see giants emerging; and the dwarves croak like frogs:

"The world has returned to savagery. What science and education have created is being destroyed by the new primitives. We are now like the prehistoric cave dwellers. Nothing distinguishes us from them save our machines of destruction and our improved techniques of slaughter."

Thus speak those who measure the world's conscience by their own. They measure the range of all Existence by the tiny span of their individual being. As if the sun did not exist but for their warmth, as if the sea was created for them to wash their feet.

—TM-ST-99

Secrets

My heart, keep secret your love,
  and hide the secret from those you see
  and you will have better fortune.
He who reveals secrets is considered a fool;
  silence and secrecy are much better for him
  who falls in love.

—MS-76

Seed

The seed which
The ripe date contains in its
Heart is the secret of the palm
Tree from the beginning of all
Creation.

—T-374

Segregation

A God Who is good knows of no segregation amongst words or names, and were a God to deny His blessing to those who pursue a different path to eternity, then there is no human who should offer worship.

—SH-T-142

Self

Man is empowered by God to hope and hope fervently, until that for which he is hoping takes the cloak of oblivion from his eyes, whereupon he will at last view his real self. And he who sees his real self sees the truth of real life for himself, for all humanity, and for all things.

—SH-T-140

It is vain for the wayfarer to knock upon the door of the empty house. Man is standing mutely between the nonexistence within him and the reality of his surroundings. If we did not possess what we have within ourselves we could not have the things we call our environs.

—SH-T-145

Self-Expression

Is it not true, that every time we draw Beauty we approach a step nearer to Beauty? And every time we write the Truth we become one with it? Or do you propose to muzzle poets and artists? Is not self-expression a deeply seated need in the human soul?

—KG-P-95

Self-Knowledge

Know your own true worth, and you shall not perish. Reason is your light and your beacon of Truth. Reason is the source of Life. God has given you Knowledge, so that by its light you may not only worship him, but also see yourself in your weakness and strength.

—WM-ST-55

Senses

How ignorant are those who see, without question, the abstract existence with *some* of their senses, but insist upon doubting until that existence reveals itself to *all* their senses. Is not faith the sense of the heart as truly as sight is the sense of the eye? And how narrow is the one who hears the song of the blackbird and sees it hovering above the branches, but doubts that which he has seen and heard until he seizes the bird with his hands. Were not a *portion* of his senses sufficient? How strange is the one who dreams in truth of a beautiful reality, and then, when he endeavours to fashion it into form but cannot succeed, doubts the dream and blasphemes the reality and distrusts the beauty!

—SH-T-148

Sex

The most highly sexed beings upon the planet are the creators, the poets, sculptors, painters, musicians . . . and so it has been from the beginning. And among them sex is a beautiful and exalted gift. Sex is always beautiful, and it is always shy.

—MS-94—95

Shadows

How unjust to themselves are those who turn their backs to the sun, and see naught except the shadows of their physical selves upon the earth!

—SH-T-150

Shepherd

In the city the best of
Man is but one of a flock, led by
The shepherd in strong voice. And he
Who follows not the command must soon
Stand before his killers.

—T-361

Sight

Not all of us are enabled to see with our inner eyes the great depths of life, and it is cruel to demand that the weak-sighted see the dim and the far.

—SH-T-129

Silence

Great truth that transcends Nature does not pass from one being to another by way of human speech. Truth chooses Silence to convey her meaning to loving souls.

—WM-ST-75

There is something greater and purer than what the mouth utters. Silence illuminates our souls, whispers to our hearts, and brings them together. Silence separates us from ourselves, makes us sail the firmament of spirit, and brings us closer to Heaven; it makes us feel that bodies are no more than prisons and that this world is only a place of exile.

—BW-ST-48

Sin

Perfection is not for the pure of soul;
There may be virtue in sin.

—MS-75

Sincerity

Many a time I have made a comparison between nobility of sacrifice and happiness of rebellion to find out which one is nobler and more beautiful; but until now I have distilled only one truth out of the whole matter, and this truth is sincerity, which makes all our deeds beautiful and honorable.

—BW-ST-117

Slavery

I accompanied the ages from the banks of the Kange to the shores of Euphrates; from the mouth of the Nile to the plains of Assyria; from the arenas of Athens to the churches of Rome; from the slums of Constantinople to the palaces of

Alexandria. . . . Yet I saw slavery moving over all, in a glorious and majestic procession of ignorance. I saw the people sacrificing the youths and maidens at the feet of the idol, calling her the God; pouring wine and perfume upon her feet, and calling her the Queen; burning incense before her image, and calling her the Prophet; kneeling and worshipping before her, and calling her the Law; fighting and dying for her, and calling her Patriotism; submitting to her will, and calling her the Shadow of God on earth; destroying and demolishing homes and institutions for her sake, and calling her Fraternity; struggling and stealing and working for her, and calling her Fortune and Happiness; killing for her, and calling her Equality.

She possesses various names, but one reality. She has many appearances, but is made of one element. In truth, she is an everlasting ailment bequeathed by each generation unto its successor.

—SH-T-64

They tell me: If you see a slave sleeping, do not wake
  him lest he be dreaming of freedom.
I tell them: If you see a slave sleeping, wake him and
  explain to him freedom.

—MS-72

Sleep

Life is but a sleep disturbed
  By dreaming, prompted by the will;
The saddened soul with sadness hides
  Its secrets, and the gay, with thrill.

—P-42

Sobriety

Few on this earth who savor life,
    And are not bored by its free gifts;
Or divert not its streams to cups
    In which their fancy floats and drifts.

Should you then find a sober soul
    Amidst this state of revelry,
Marvel how a moon did find
    In this rain cloud a canopy.

—P-37

Society

Society
Is of naught but clamour and woe
And strife. She is but the web of
The spider, the tunnel of the mole.

—T-376

Solitude

The sorrowful spirit finds relaxation in solitude. It abhors people, as a wounded deer deserts the herd and lives in a cave until it is healed or dead.

—BW-ST-87

Solitude has soft, silky hands, but with strong fingers it grasps the heart and makes it ache with sorrow. Solitude is the ally of sorrow as well as a companion of spiritual exaltation.

—BW-ST-19

Your life, my brother, is a solitary habitation separated from other men's dwellings. It is a house into whose interior no neighbor's gaze can penetrate. If it were plunged into darkness, your neighbor's lamp could not illumine it. If it were emptied of provisions, the stores of your neighbors could not fill it. If it stood in a desert, you could not move it into other men's gardens, tilled and planted by other hands. If it stood on a mountaintop, you could not bring it down into the valley trod by other men's feet.

Your spirit's life, my brother, is encompassed by loneliness, and were it not for that loneliness and solitude, you would not be *you*, nor would I be *I*. Were it not for this loneliness and solitude, I would come to believe on hearing your voice that it was my voice speaking; or seeing your face, that it was myself looking into a mirror.

—WM-ST-43

Song

Give to me the reed and sing thou!
For the song is gracious shade,
And the plaint of reed remaineth
When illusions dim and fade.

—P-39

Sorrow

Sorrow is the shadow of a God who
Lives not in the domain of evil hearts.

—SH-T-86

Sorrow, if able to speak, would
Prove sweeter than the joy of song.

—SH-T-99

He who has not looked on Sorrow will never see Joy.

—WM-ST-88

The sorrowful spirit finds rest when united with a similar one. They join affectionately, as a stranger is cheered when he sees another stranger in a strange land. Hearts that are united through the medium of sorrow will not be separated by the glory of happiness.

—BW-ST-42

The secret of the heart is encased
In sorrow, and only in sorrow is
Found our joy, while happiness serves
But to conceal the deep mystery of life.

—T-362

Soul

The reason why the soul exists
Is folded in the soul itself;
No painting could its essence show,
Nor manifest its real self.

—P-65

The soul does not see anything in life save that which is in the soul itself. It does not believe except in its own private event, and when it experiences something, the outcome becomes a part of it.

—SP-ST-56

Sounds of Nature

When the birds sing, do they call to the flowers in the fields, or are they speaking to the trees, or are they echoing the murmur of the brooks? For Man with his understanding cannot know what the bird is saying, nor what the brook is murmuring, nor what the waves whisper when they touch the beaches slowly and gently.

Man with his understanding cannot know what the rain

is saying when it falls upon the leaves of the trees or when it taps at the window panes. He cannot know what the breeze is saying to the flowers in the fields.

But the Heart of Man can feel and grasp the meaning of these sounds that play upon his feelings. Eternal Wisdom often speaks to him in a mysterious language; Soul and Nature converse together, while Man stands speechless and bewildered.

Yet has not Man wept at the sounds? And are not his tears eloquent understanding?

—WM-ST-58

Spirit

The spirit in every being is made manifest in the eyes, the countenance, and in all bodily movements and gestures. Our appearance, our words, our actions are never greater than ourselves. For the soul is our house; our eyes its windows; and our words its messengers.

—WM-ST-62

The strength of the spirit alone is
The power of powers, and must in time
Crumble to powder all things opposing
It. Do not condemn, but pity the
Faithless and their weakness and their
Ignorance and their nothingness.

—T-365

Through the spirit,
Not the body, love must be shown,
As it is to enliven, not to deaden,
That the wine is pressed.

—T-371

You may deprive me of my possessions; you may shed my blood and burn my body, but you cannot hurt my spirit or touch my truth.

—S

Spirits

Between the people of eternity and people of the earth there is a constant communication, and all comply with the will of that unseen power. Oftentimes an individual will perform an act, believing that it is born of his own free will, accord, and command, but in fact he is being guided and impelled with precision to do it. Many great men attained their glory by surrendering themselves in complete submission to the will of the spirit, employing no reluctance or resistance to its demands, as a violin surrenders itself to the complete will of a fine musician.

Between the spiritual world and the world of substance there is a path upon which we walk in a swoon of slumber. It reaches us and we are unaware of its strength, and when we return to ourselves we find that we are carrying with our real hands the seeds to be planted carefully in the good earth of our daily lives, bringing forth good deeds and words of beauty. Were it not for that path between our lives and the departed lives, no prophet or poet or learned man would have appeared among the people.

—SH-T-146

Spiritual Affinity

It is wrong to think that love comes from long companionship and persevering courtship. Love is the offspring of spiritual affinity and unless that affinity is created in a moment, it will not be created in years or even generations.

—BW-ST-52

Spiritual Awakening

Spiritual awakening is the most essential thing in man's life, and it is the sole purpose of being. Is not civilization, in all its tragic forms, a supreme motive for spiritual awakening? Then how can we deny existing matter, while its very existence is unwavering proof of its conformability into the intended fitness? The present civilization may possess a vanishing purpose, but the eternal law has offered to that purpose a ladder whose steps can lead to a free substance.

—SH-T-29

Spirituality

Time and place are spiritual states, and all that is seen and heard is spiritual. If you close your eyes you will perceive all things through the depths of your inner self, and you will see the world physical and ethereal, in its intended entirety, and you will acquaint yourself with its necessary laws and precautions, and you will understand the greatness that it possesses beyond its closeness.

—SH-T-139

Spring

In every winter's heart there is a quivering spring, and behind the veil of each night there is a smiling dawn.

—SP-ST-57

Strength

The very strength that protects the heart from injury is the strength that prevents the heart from enlarging to its intended greatness within. The song of the voice is sweet, but the song of the heart is the pure voice of heaven.

—SH-T-121

Submission

Men, even if they are born free, will remain slaves of strict laws enacted by their forefathers; and the firmament, which we imagine as unchanging, is the yielding of today to the will of tomorrow and submission of yesterday to the will of today.

—BW-ST-118

Sword

Whoever reaches eternity with sword in his hand lives as long as there is justice.

—MS-29

Sympathy

The sympathy that touches the neighbour's heart is more supreme than the hidden virtue in the unseen corners of the convent. A word of compassion to the weak criminal or prostitute is nobler than the long prayer which we repeat emptily every day in the temple.

—SR-T-257

T

Talk

I am bored with gabbers and their gab; my soul abhors them. . . .

Is there in this universe a nook where I can go and live happily by myself?

Is there any place where there is no traffic in empty talk?

Is there on this earth one who does not worship himself talking?

Is there any person among all persons whose mouth is not a hiding place for the knavish Mister Gabber?

—TM-ST-40-42

Teacher

Whoever would be a teacher of men let him begin by teaching himself before teaching others; and let him teach by example before teaching by word. For he who teaches himself and rectifies his own ways is more deserving of respect and reverence than he who would teach others and rectify their ways.

—KG-P-27

Tears

He who is seared and cleansed once with his
Own tears will remain pure forevermore.

—SH-T-86

The tears you shed are purer than the laughter of him
that seeks to forget and sweeter than the mockery of the
scoffer. These tears cleanse the heart of the blight of hatred,
and teach man to share the pain of the brokenhearted. They
are the tears of the Nazarene.

—WM-ST-65

Love that is cleansed by tears will remain eternally pure
and beautiful.

—BW-ST-42

The tears of young men are the overflow of full hearts.
But the tears of old men are the residue of age dropping
upon their cheeks, the remains of life in weakened bodies.
Tears in the eyes of young men resemble drops of dew upon
a rose, but the tears of old men resemble yellow autumn
leaves, blown and scattered by the wind as the winter of life
approaches.

—S

Tears and Laughter

I would not exchange the laughter of my heart for the
fortunes of the multitudes; nor would I be content with con-
verting my tears, invited by my agonized self, into calm. It
is my fervent hope that my whole life on this earth will ever
be tears and laughter.

—T-413

Teeth

In the mouth of Society are many diseased teeth, decayed to the bones of the jaws. But Society makes no efforts to have them extracted and be rid of the affliction. It contents itself with gold fillings. Many are the dentists who treat the decayed teeth of Society with glittering gold.

Numerous are those who yield to the enticements of such reformers, and pain, sickness, and death are their lot. . . .

Visit the courts and witness the acts of the crooked and corrupted purveyors of justice. *See* how they play with the thoughts and minds of the simple people as a cat plays with a mouse.

Visit the homes of the rich where conceit, falsehood, and hypocrisy reign.

But don't neglect to go through the huts of the poor as well, where dwell fear, ignorance, and cowardice.

Then visit the nimble-fingered dentists, possessors of delicate instruments, dental plasters and tranquilizers, who spend their days filling the cavities in the rotten teeth of the nation to mask the decay.

—TM-ST-38

Things

Substantial things deaden a man without suffering; love awakens him with enlivening pains.

—TL-T-3

If your knowledge teaches you not the value of things, and frees you not from the bondage to matter, you shall never come near the throne of Truth.

—WM-ST-63

Thirst

The thirst of soul is sweeter than the wine of material things, and the fear of spirit is dearer than the security of the body.

—BW-ST-69

Throng

Life amid the throngs is but brief
And drug-laden slumber, mixed with
Mad dreams and spectres and fears.

—T-362

Time

This world is but a winery,
    Its host and master Father Time,
Who caters only to those steep'd
    In dreams discordant, without rhyme.

For people drink and race as though
    They were the steeds of mad desire;
Thus some are blatant when they pray,
    And others frenzied to acquire.

—P-39

The people
Of the city abuse the wine of Time,
For they think upon it as a temple,
And they drink of it with ease and
With unthinking, and they flee,
Scurrying into old age with deep
But unknowing sorrow.

—T-363

How strange Time is, and how queer we are! Time has really changed, and lo, it has changed us too. It walked one step forward, unveiled its face, alarmed us and then elated us.

Yesterday we complained about Time and trembled at its terrors. But today we have learned to love it and revere it, for we now understand its intents, its natural disposition, its secrets, and its mysteries.

Yesterday we crawled in fright like shuddering ghosts between the fears of the night and the menaces of the day. But today we walk joyously towards the mountain peak, the dwelling place of the raging tempest and the birthplace of thunder. . . .

Yesterday we honored false prophets and sorcerers. But today Time has changed, and lo, it has changed us too. We can now stare at the face of the sun and listen to the songs of the sea, and nothing can shake us except a cyclone.

Yesterday we tore down the temples of our souls and from their debris we built tombs for our forefathers. But today our souls have turned into sacred altars that the ghosts of the past cannot approach, that the fleshless fingers of the dead cannot touch.

We were a silent thought hidden in the corners of Oblivion. Today we are a strong voice that can make the firmament reverberate.

—TM-ST-33

Torch

The human soul is but a part of a burning torch which God separated from Himself at Creation.

—WM-ST-67

Treasure

Knowledge and understanding are life's faithful companions who will never prove untrue to you. For knowledge is your crown, and understanding your staff; and when they are with you, you can possess no greater treasures.

—WM-ST-62

Truth

Truth is like the stars; it does not appear except from behind obscurity of the night. Truth is like all beautiful things in the world; it does not disclose its desirability except to those who first feel the influence of falsehood. Truth is a deep kindness that teaches us to be content in our everyday life and share with the people the same happiness.

—SR-T-255

He who would seek truth and proclaim it to mankind is bound to suffer. My sorrows have taught me to understand the sorrows of my fellow men . . . persecution . . . [has not] dimmed the vision within me.

—VM-P-86

Truth calls to us, drawn by the innocent laughter of a child, or the kiss of a loved one; but we close the doors of affection in her face and deal with her as with an enemy.

—WM-ST-47

U

Unawareness

The human heart cries out for help; the human soul implores us for deliverance; but we do not heed their cries, for we neither hear nor understand. But the man who hears and understands we call mad, and flee from him.

Thus the nights pass, and we live in unawareness; and the days greet us and embrace us. But we live in constant dread of day and night.

—WM-ST-47

Unseen

The subtlest beauties in our life are unseen and unheard.

—SP-ST-30

The Jews, my beloved, awaited the coming of a Messiah, who had been promised them, and who was to deliver them from bondage.

And the Great Soul of the World sensed that the worship of Jupiter and Minerva no longer availed, for the thirsty hearts of men could not be quenched with that wine.

In Rome men pondered the divinity of Apollo, a god

without pity, and the beauty of Venus already fallen into decay.

For deep in their hearts, though they did not understand it, these nations hungered and thirsted for the supreme teaching that would transcend any to be found on the earth. They yearned for the spirit's freedom that would teach man to rejoice with his neighbor at the light of the sun and the wonder of living. For it is this cherished freedom that brings man close to the Unseen, which he can approach without fear or shame.

—WM-ST-92

V

Virgin

There is no secret in the mystery of life stronger and more beautiful than that attachment which converts the silence of a virgin's spirit into a perpetual awareness that makes a person forget the past, for it kindles fiercely in the heart the sweet and overwhelming hope of the coming future.

—SR-T-264

W

War

You are my brother, but why are you quarreling with me?
Why do you invade my country and try to subjugate me for
the sake of pleasing those who are seeking glory and authority?

Why do you leave your wife and children and follow
Death to the distant land for the sake of those who buy
glory with your blood, and high honour with your mother's
tears?

Is it an honour for a man to kill his brother man? If you
deem it an honour, let it be an act of worship, and erect a
temple to Cain who slew his brother Abel.

—TL-T-7

Can lovers meet and exchange kisses on battlefields still
acrid with bomb fumes?

Will the poet compose his songs under stars veiled in
gun smoke?

Will the musician strum his lute in a night whose silence
was ravished by terror?

—TM-ST-98

Way to God

Perhaps we are nearer to Him each time we try to divide Him and find Him indivisible. Yet do I say that art, through drawing a line between the beautiful and the ugly, is the nearest way to God. Pure meditation is another way. But it leads to silence and to self-confinement. Silence is truer and more expressive than speech; and the hour shall come when we shall be silent. But why muzzle our tongues before that hour has struck? There is your friend Lao Tze; he became silent, but when? After he gave to the world the gist of his faith in words.

—KG-P-96

Weakness

That deed which in our guilt we today call weakness, will appear tomorrow as an essential link in the complete chain of Man.

—WM-ST-32

Wealth

In some countries, the parent's wealth is a source of misery for the children. The wide strong box which the father and mother together have used for the safety of their wealth becomes a narrow, dark prison for the souls of their heirs. The Almighty Dinar which the people worship becomes a demon which punishes the spirit and deadens the heart.

—BW-ST-64

Will

To Will belongs the Right. For Souls
    When strong prevail, when weak become
Subject to changes, good and bad,
    And with the wind may go and come.

Then, deny not that Will in Soul
Is greater than the Might of Arm,
And weakling only mounts the throne
Of those beyond the good and harm.

—P-50

Wings

God has given you a spirit with wings on which to soar into the spacious firmament of Love and Freedom. Is it not pitiful then that you cut your wings with your own hands and suffer your soul to crawl like an insect upon the earth?

—WM-ST-67

Wisdom

The wise man is he who loves and reveres God. A man's merit lies in his knowledge and in his deeds, not in his color, faith, race, or descent. For remember, my friend, the son of a shepherd who possesses knowledge is of greater worth to a nation than the heir to the throne, if he be ignorant. Knowledge is your true patent of nobility, no matter who your father or what your race may be.

—WM-ST-61

Keep me away from the wisdom which does not cry, the philosophy which does not laugh and the greatness which does not bow before children.

—MS-72

Woman

A woman whom Providence has provided with beauty of spirit and body is a truth, at the same time both open and secret, which we understand only by love, and touch only by virtue; and when we attempt to describe such a woman she disappears like a vapor.

—BW-ST-39

Women opened the windows of my eyes and the doors of my spirit. Had it not been for the woman-mother, the woman-sister, and the woman-friend, I would have been sleeping among those who seek the tranquility of the world with their snoring.

—SP-P-31

Writers and poets try to understand the truth about woman. But until this day they have never understood her heart because, looking upon her through the veil of desire, they see nothing except the shape of her body. Or they look upon her through a magnifying glass of spite and find nothing in her but weakness and submission.

—S

Woman's Heart
A woman's heart will not change with time or season; even if it dies eternally, it will never perish. A woman's heart is like a field turned into a battleground; after the trees are uprooted and the grass is burned and the rocks are reddened with blood and the earth is planted with bones and skulls, it is calm and silent as if nothing has happened; for the spring and autumn come at their intervals and resume their work.

—BW-ST-71

Words
Wisdom is not in words;
Wisdom is meaning within words.

—MS-74

Worship

God does not like to be worshipped by an ignorant man who imitates someone else.

—SR-T-267

Worth

If your knowledge teaches you not to rise above human weakness and misery and lead your fellow man on the right path, you are indeed a man of little worth and will remain such till Judgment Day.

—WM-ST-63

Writer

Are you a writer who holds his head high above the crowd, while his brain is deep in the abyss of the past, that is filled with the tatters and useless cast-offs of the ages? If so, you are like a stagnant pool of water.

Or are you the keen thinker, who scrutinizes his inner self, discarding that which is useless, outworn and evil, but preserving that which is useful and good? If so, you are as manna to the hungry, and as cool, clear water to the thirsty.

—WM-ST-36

Y

Youth

Youth is a beautiful dream, on whose brightness books shed a blinding dust. Will ever the day come when the wise link the joy of knowledge to youth's dream? Will ever the day come when Nature becomes the teacher of man, humanity his book and life his school? Youth's joyous purpose cannot be fulfilled until that day comes. Too slow is our march toward spiritual elevation, because we make so little use of youth's ardor.

—TM-ST-55

Beauty belongs to youth, but the youth for whom this earth was made is naught but a dream whose sweetness is enslaved to a blindness that renders its awareness too late. Will ever the day come when the wise will band together the sweet dreams of youth and the joy of knowledge? Each is but naught when in solitary existence.

—T-302

Youth and Age

Mankind divided into two long columns, one composed of the aged and bent, who support themselves on crooked

staves, and as they walk on the path of Life, they pant as if
they were climbing toward a mountaintop, while they are
actually descending into the abyss.

And the second column is composed of youth, running
as with winged feet, singing as if their throats were strung
with silver strings, and climbing toward the mountaintop
as though drawn by some irresistible, magic power.

—WM-ST-36

Until when shall the people remain asleep?
Until when shall they continue to glorify those
Who attained greatness by moments of advantage?
How long shall they ignore those who enable
Them to see the beauty of their spirit,
Symbol of peace and love?
Until when shall human beings honor the dead
And forget the living, who spend their lives
Encircled in misery, and who consume themselves
Like burning candles to illuminate the way
For the ignorant and lead them into the path of light?

—TL-T-300